Filing Order

Sonnets
by

John Delaney

Finishing Line Press
Georgetown, Kentucky

Filing Order

Copyright © 2025 by John Delaney
ISBN 979-8-88838-948-5 First Edition
All rights reserved under International and Pan-American Copyright Conventions. No part of this book may be reproduced in any manner whatsoever without written permission from the publisher, except in the case of brief quotations embodied in critical articles and reviews.

Publisher: Leah Huete de Maines
Editor: Christen Kincaid
Cover Art: John Delaney
Author Photo: Evelyn van Naerssen
Cover Design: Elizabeth Maines McCleavy

Order online: www.finishinglinepress.com
also available on amazon.com

Author inquiries and mail orders:
Finishing Line Press
PO Box 1626
Georgetown, Kentucky 40324
USA

Contents

Filing Order 1

Ancestry.Com(mon) 2
At the Equator 3
Best Laid Plans 4
Boulder 5
Boy in a Boatneck Shirt and Clam Diggers 6
Breaking Points 7
Cat Philosophy 8
Continental Divide 9
The Country Club Set 10
Cremation 11
The Domino Effect 12
Downsizing 13
The Elephant with the Bright White Toenails 14
Entering Wyoming, 1961 15
Farewell Tour 16
The Foal 17
Giddy Up 18
A Glass of Water 19
The Good Humor Man 20
Handwriting on the Wall 21
The House That Jo and Martin Built 22
Hush 23
James Cook's Window 24
Kindness 25
Laundry 26
Leafcutter Ants Promenade 27
Less Than 1% 28
Let Me Tell You What I Think 29
The Letter 30

Low Tide Island	31
Meteorologic	32
The Mouse Trap	33
My Turn	34
Newborn	35-36
October Sunflowers	37
Paperweights	38
Pearly Gates	39
Poem as Map	40
Rain Stick	41
Riding an E-Bike at Seventy	42
Scenic Views	43
Sea Glass	44
Selected Bibliography	45
Situations Wanted	46
So Much Sadness/Sorrow Coming	47
Symptoms	48
Throwing Out My Mother's Slides	49
To the End	50
Two Photos (1951, 2010)	51
Walking the Shelter Dogs	52
The Weight of Love	53
When I Grow Up (Since You Asked)	54
Windrose	55
Wishing Stone	56
You	57
Acknowledgments	58
Author Biography / About This Book	59

To Jo and Martin

In truth, the prison, unto which we doom
Ourselves, no prison is: and hence to me,
In sundry moods, 'twas pastime to be bound
Within the Sonnet's scanty plot of ground:
Pleased if some Souls (for such there needs must be)
Who have felt the weight of too much liberty,
Should find short solace there, as I have found.

  —from "A Prefatory Sonnet"
   by William Wordsworth (1770-1850)

Filing Order

Nothing before something.
Numbers before letters.
Desire, friendship, love.

Punctuation as space.
Text as uppercase.
SERF, SIR, ST PETER.

From left to right,
top to bottom.
Form follows function.

Age before beauty.
Honor before glory.
Character, setting, story.

Thou before though.

Yes before no.

Ancestry.Com(mon)

You spit into a test tube
and mail it to a lab
to learn where you came from
thousands of years ago,
plotting the caravan route
of your ancestors
out of Africa, Planet Earth.

But if atoms could be tagged,
from which star's collapse,
now light years away,
were itty-bitty pieces
grab-bagged for your DNA?
To think you've come so far—
to be another star's birth.

At the Equator
    Mitad del Mundo, Ecuador

You straddle a red line in the pavement
and inhabit two hemispheres
for a moment, or is that your brain
I'm really talking about, how thoughts
and feelings swirl in opposite directions
depending on your mental whereabouts.

The guide was pretty sure about it,
demonstrating, with a kitchen sink
on legs and a pail of water, each side
of the proverbial line. We were wowed
by what appeared to be a magic trick.

In our photo, my son and I link arms
across. Later, we learned from GPS
the true equator still lay north of us.

Best Laid Plans

Somewhere between 'oh, no' and 'oh, well'
the verdict falls: you won't have any kids.

I watched a show on endangered penguins
that yearly breed in a South African town
and make their nests among residents' homes,
under shrubs and hedges, off of side streets.

One pair of newlyweds chose a culvert
with a protective concrete ceiling.
But then, a sudden summer downpour
came rushing through, driving them down the hill.

When they got back, their nest and eggs were gone.
They briefly reassessed, then waddled off,
disabused of their parental notion.
Already, they felt drawn to the ocean.

Boulder

The thing is, he doesn't complain—
'Why are we following the same trail we took yesterday?'
(And, I might add, the day before that, too.)

Perhaps he doesn't notice, but of course he does.
He just doesn't care! Part pit bull, part sweetheart,
he plods along as if there is no déjà vu.

He still wants to smell the plants and pee
in the right places. It's all as interesting
as it ever was. The path deserves its due.

I have to admire his performance:
a smell, a poke, a glance. Progress is slow.
The leash often limits what he wants to pursue.

But when we get back, I've been converted
by his shrugged-approach to life's repetitions: make them new.

Boy in a Boatneck Shirt and Clam Diggers

I wore them everywhere when I was ten:
vertical stripes of black, gold, white, and red,
with long white shorts. We lived far from the ocean
so there was nothing nautical to pretend.

My sisters were modish teenagers,
of a more fashionable age,
insisting you are what you wear.
I swear they had their hands in it.

Too nice to climb trees, but I did.
Too bright for hide-and-seek, but I hid.
I felt dashing and daring
but a little desperate perhaps,

adding cowboy boots to the "outfit." Boy,
boyhood's tough to wear: I grew out of it.

Breaking Points

To love a tree that you planted,
watching it grow above you,
spreading shade with clusters of leaves,
is not nothing to take for granted;
it will last a long time, ringed with hope,
longer than your heart grieves
its passing seasons too.

But to love something that doesn't live long—
the little boy in your son,
who played with his truck toy
alone in his room, so grown and gone;
or Tug, the cat that, gently with a paw,
would touch your face in bed and then 'meow'—
those precious moments break you now.

Cat Philosophy

There's always that wide-eyed stare
piercing everything that moves.
A tilt of the head to get perspective.
Then there's that sudden swipe of paw
to snag a fleeting piece of something
before it's gone—but letting go.
There's plenty of time to sleep
to mull the memories over.
And a few words sparingly spoken
to get the point across, the need known;
easy assent and approval
expressed in the patois of purring.

Keep the body clean, a curious mind.
Scratch the years behind.

Continental Divide

When we divvied up our lifetime
together, you got the furniture;
I took some rare books and vintage maps.
You kept your family's Indonesian trunk;
I, my mother's Yankee mantel clock.
All in all, we split it down the middle,
after discarding all the junk
we had collected to outfit the years.
There were plenty of good memories,
handfuls, in fact, to cushion the boxes.

Yesterday, in my Subaru burro
I crossed the Continental Divide,
where, as you know, water is pulled
either east or west. Even tears.

The Country Club Set
    Apologies to L. P. Hartley

The past is a private country club.
We knew someone who knew someone
and secured sustaining memberships.
(We lost our patience on the waiting list.)
The dues are pretty stiff, but we can choose
with whom to fraternize: the exclusive
few, our privileged peers, or some better born.

Often, we'd rather hobnob there than here—
to sit out on the greenside patio
in the early evening's shadowed light
and watch the last group's approaching shots.
To toast our handicaps with hearty laughs
and clink the glasses all around.
Wet-eyed Old Boys. Twinkle-eyed Chaps.

Cremation

We watched the pine box enter,
the door close,
and then the jets of the burners roared.
'Through hell he goes,'

I thought. And how we stood
together silently,
hearing the flames consume
so violently

the stoic man that was our dad.
It wouldn't take long
to reduce his 90 years to ashes,
everything he held right or wrong.

I like to think we felt a modicum of warmth disperse
across the cold, unloving universe.

The Domino Effect

No doubt you've seen those large layered layouts
of colored dominoes that snake and spin
up stairs and over constructed landscapes,
or run in parallel tracks or flower
or spiral or fork in dizzying routes,
cascading forward with unwavering,
resolute determination, rushing
ahead wherever the patterns take them,
not one misstep to stop the process cold,
but all unified in a march of time,
as if being pushed by constant pressure
on their backs, and never looking behind.

As they approach the end, you gain the view—

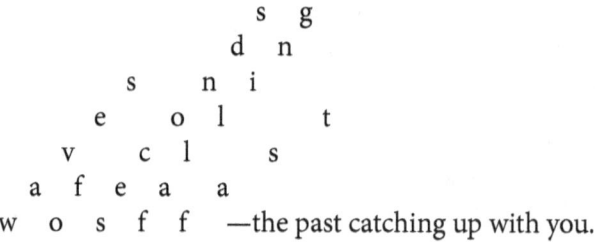

```
                          s     g
                       d     n
                 s     n     i
              e     o     l           t
           v     c     l        s
        a     f     e     a        a
     w     o     s     f     f    —the past catching up with you.
```

Downsizing

The four-bedroom house is now a one-floor two.
I cut the grass with an old hand mower.
We don't have a basement to store regrets
and tend to keep the thermostat lower.
Once our Labradors died, we forswore all pets.

Bookcases of novels and biographies
render their reading to cable channels.
My Oxford shirts and sharp-creased khakis
were bagged to Goodwill for jeans and flannels.

My socks, all black, are interchangeable.
Our double bed begat twin mattresses.
We thumb our address book, not the Bible.

And love, my only Earth—where wild guesses
still come true—I remember less and less of you.

The Elephant with the Bright White Toenails
Oregon Zoo, Portland

In the dust of her summer days,
trudging with the whole troop
of her adopted family
from feeding lot to waterhole
in the expanded enclosure,
swaying with measured steps
as elephants do, trunk curled up,
her large ear flaps sweeping the air
like paper fans in the hampered heat,
I see this orphan they named Chendra
as the calf she once had been,
just a little girl with ponytails
and pink ribbons and party dress,
so proud of her bright white toenails.

Chendra is the only Bornean elephant living in North America.

Entering Wyoming, 1961

We straddle the state sign. Mom takes the shot:
four kids on a cross-country road trip.
I'm almost eleven; my oldest sister
will graduate from college next year.
All of us are rarin' to be somewhere else,
but Mom has corralled us for nine weeks:
a final roundup before time's slaughter.

There's a frisky breeze that ruffles our hair,
while the clouds in the distance horse around.
We smile meekly before the mountains.
"You'll never forget these things," she says,
promising me cowboy boots in Cheyenne.
Soon nature calls: the future wants our lives.
We get back in the car, and mother drives.

Farewell Tour

Gradually, the rock bands of the Sixties
announce their final concert tours
as their members turn wistful and eighty.
They try to salvage that early glory
one more time for us, the loyal fans
who, having followed their tabloid story,
will pay anything to see them perform
the music that we carry in our heads.

I'm reminded of the little girl
I saw holding her mommy's hand
in the local grocery's produce aisle.
She turned to look at me, then smiled and waved,
as they retreated into the store.
She'd already begun her farewell tour.

The Foal
> *Scientists find perfectly preserved ancient foal in Siberia . . . younger than two weeks when it apparently drowned in mud . . .estimated to be 42,000 years old.*
> —CNN

The day a workman carried you out of the crater in his arms,
all gangly legs, with matted hair still brown,
perfectly preserved in the permafrost,
it seemed that you had just been born.

But not to an age tusked by woolly mammoths,
nor manhandled by implements of stone.
You were destined for more gallantry than that.
That past has thawed: you've come into your own.

The stocky Mongol horses of the Steppes,
the thoroughbreds of bluegrass Kentucky,
and every saddled workhorse in-between—
if they could race, with nostrils flaring, back through time,

their pounding hooves would herald your grand story:
how you became their speed and strength and glory.

Giddy Up

Chronic lower back pain
keeps me sleeping on my side.
Calcium buildup in my shoulder
restricts its sphere of action
to what I can gingerly bear.
Eye drops at night fend off glaucoma.
Blood vessels are breaking under the skin . . .

Mild cases, to be sure, of my aging.
So far I've dodged the bullets.
But garbed bandana bandits
are closing in on my stagecoach.
Can I hold the reins long enough
to get where I'm going?
I giddy up without knowing.

A Glass of Water

So clear, it seems empty at first,
till I bring it to my lips
in slow and steady sips
to quench my thirst.

Thus, as I drink,
a transfer is taking place
within a larger space.
That's what I think

when I hold the glass
empty now
that had been full: how
water will pass

so seamlessly, seem-lessly,
just as *is* becomes *was* does.

The Good Humor Man

So, after supper, on a summer night,
my grade school friends, shrieking in the street,
were running across the grass between our yards,
congregating around a truck so white,

and I'd press my dad if there was money
for a cone, 'please', dipped in milk chocolate,
as he fished in his pants' pocket for change
and asked for a toasted almond, 'Johnny'.

In my graying years, what turns back the clock
is the summons of that Pied Piper's bell,
when joyous spontaneity followed
in magnetic motion around the block.

When I was a kid in a neighborhood.
When my father was a good humor man.

Handwriting on the Wall

We called my father's writing chicken scratch.
Arrhythmic waves of an EKG
ran rapid and jagged along the page.
His white-collar work made rough numbers talk
by talking tough, the way accountants do,
with sleeves rolled up in glass-walled offices.
He wore striped ties with a crouched tiger's rage.

My mother's cursive was flowing and vibrant
as her embroideries of state flowers,
buoyant and boisterous, so clean and crisp.
Taught in school the basics on lined paper,
she looped above and below its fence rails,
coaxing letters towards the horizon
in sentences of pampered penmanship.

The House That Jo and Martin Built

I live in the house that my parents built,
a tiny home I kept expanding,
though I followed their philosophy:
a strong foundation, good plumbing,
and a warranted weatherproof roof.

The maintenance costs have been high
and time-consuming. It came unfurnished.
I didn't find my style for many years,
and am reluctant now to make more changes.
Nature is claiming my exterior.

What they left behind were basic blueprints.
Though I lacked the skills of a contractor
to construct this life with just fingerprints,
hand tools of love made up the difference.

Hush

The fawn stood in the middle of the trail,
stiffly scanning its surroundings,
having just emerged from ferns
under trees that were thick and lush,
into the spotlight of the sun,
where all were alerted to each other.

We stopped, and with a gentle call
brought it homing towards us in a rush.
But it stopped, too, some yards away.
Clearly, we were not what it expected,
and no name could draw it any closer.
Soon it sought the embrace of the brush.

Moral: when innocence approaches, seeking
signs of recognition, nature cries 'hush'.

James Cook's Window (Whitby, England)

Aye, it's a good view of the River Esk
from the attic of the Grape Lane house
where young James Cook lived as an apprentice
and confronted his maritime doubts.

There were always ships in the harbor
plying the East coast coal-carrying trade,
being built, and repaired and outfitted—
aye, there, many a seaman was made.

How his future was framed by this window!
How it teased him to set sail on the sea
and to trust in the wind's promise to blow.

You wonder what glory he must have seen,
a boy, who began the life of a sailor
on a ship named *Freelove*, at eighteen.

Endeavour, *the ship Cook captained on his first circumnavigation of the globe, was built in Whitby.*

Kindness

A chickadee has found the feeder: word
spreads fast in its community, sharing
the good fortune. Even sparrows have heard
the news and come curious to confirm.

Some grab and go quickly, relishing
a quiet moment alone with their find;
others sit and feast, furtively looking
like thieves counting their ill-gotten gains.

So much for the natural world, where
kindness can be a gift or a burden.
Though the glass is half full or half empty,
the contents are the same, the glass is clear.

Drink up, you worrywarts, lads and lasses:
time, too, is kind because it passes.

Laundry

I pull last week's laundry from the dryer:
a pair of jeans, some t-shirts and flannels,
basic cotton underwear, and a heap
of black socks, each pair a match made in heaven.
(Somehow, though, there's always an orphan.)

I was clothed like a Goodwill mannequin,
your average Joe, comfy and casual,
dressed for the demands of chores and errands,
a picnic concert, a walk on the beach.
All that was washed out of last week. And now,

who knows what I could/would/should be or do
in different clothes? Clean, fresh-smelling
is a start. I hope to come out unscathed,
no worse for wear, just a little wrinkled.

Leafcutter Ants Promenade

Verdant slices
in myriad shapes
wobble down the tree's branch,
then its trunk
and across the ground,
dropping out of sight.
All day, all night,

a sparkling chain
of emeralds move
on a wriggling bracelet—
looters making off
with a treasure trove,
Cubist artist-thieves
heisting puzzle pieces.

After humans, leafcutter ants form the next largest and most complex animal societies on Earth.

Less Than 1%
> *Over 99 percent of all species that have ever existed are extinct.*
> —Smithsonian Magazine

Similarly, out of the teeming mass
of thoughts, herds of ruminations,
subjected to the climate changes
of memory loss and faulty logic
and suffocating clouds of confusion,
escaping the predation of plagiarists
and copycats, organisms evolved:

new species of a viable idea
that survived the mass extinctions
of ignorance and stupidity
because they took refuge inside brains
that kept sparking from its insight
like a stimulant. Given raw birth
from cosmic chaos, yet they changed the Earth.

Let Me Tell You What I Think

We'll never live up to our potential.
It always comes down to greed.
And jealousy. Even lazy yoga.
What life lets you get away with.

Our actions peddle pet philosophies
around the pedestals of statued principles.
Your *modus operandi*
becomes your *raison d'être*.

We'll never be more than apprentices
in Nature's beauty salons or fabrication shops.
Oglers. Idlers. Hourly help.
You'll be lucky to get a foot in the door

or out of your mouth. We'll never learn.

Now, your turn.

The Letter

No, the bad news hasn't reached me yet,
though my body's been preparing for it.
I'd prefer it come by Pony Express.
Still, the distances have been challenging
to cross, the obstacles to overcome—
childhood, some bruises and broken bones,
foolhardy adventures, dares and dangers.

But neither snow nor rain nor heat nor gloom
keeps the postman from his appointed rounds.
He always finds my forwarding address.
The mail comes every day, mostly junk,
offering palliatives and placebos.
I wait for a signed, handwritten letter.
If it tells the truth, I might feel better.

Low Tide Island
Port Townsend, WA

Emerging this morning from the spring tide:
a barren expanse of land sometimes seen,
perhaps some fifty yards long by ten wide,
unknown to the gulls when I first spied it.

I think worry acts like this, ascending
from the depths when spirits sink below,
exposing a netherworld, offending
banality, anathema to hope.

Or is that hope has surfaced, floating
as a refuge with no requirements
for refugees, where they can safely beach
if they can reach its sand? This island

sighting had all the likelihood of rhymes
raising my poems. It happens sometimes.

Meteorologic

The day my father died, we could remark
how it wasn't a bad day weather-wise:
cloudy but comfortable—'variable skies' —
the middle of spring. It was late getting dark.

No doubt, above the clouds, the sun was shining
as it daily did, while down where prayers are said
we charted death's approach on deeper breaths
and felt the wake from them beside his bed.

That night it rained a heavy, humid rain.
Our weatherman! whose reports we learned verbatim,
earned his weatherproof rest thankfully without pain.

In the dry shelter of this interim
dead calm, each of us now starts divining
how to forecast the future without him.

The Mouse Trap

CAN'T MISS is the motto of this contrap-
tion. (Sounds like some last minute directions
to a place so obvious that a map
becomes redundant, and so do questions.)

And sure enough, this mouse had no trouble.
He lies with his nose a hair from the cheese.
You can tell he was just about to nibble
in when it was curtains! That is the tease

that kills. Would your faith match that of this mouse
if you, on your way, were led to suppose—
only to be thunderstruck by a lie?

Imagine it: your nose guides to the house;
you peek in the open door; you're so close
you have your god in sight. But damn! You die.

My Turn

We arrive at the four-way stop, then pause,
as each, by a natural protocol,
takes his turn to continue the journey.
And I'm reminded of other times
I waited for my turn, beginning
at the school playground for a chance
on the slide or swing. Or waiting on deck
at softball or in a game of potsies.

Taking turns is the fair way, and we reach
this consensus at a very young age.
You get your chance, I, mine. Patience
is the precedence we pay. So I wait
at the intersection as, one by one,
others fetch their futures. Now, it's my turn.

Newborn

Test: Positive

The test-tube test was taken this morning.
Result: a rust-colored doughnut-shaped ring.

That such a means should bring first proof of you
suggests the magic of this fragile life,
the sleight-of-love that makes the wish come true.
Yet pride insists we make a full disclosure:
you were the best laid scheme of man and wife,
in mind and body, consummate pleasure,

twice conceived. Eight months from now your crying
will prove this was no trick our bodies play.
After a year and a half of trying
the random ritual, the contrived act,
imagine our delight to learn today
you're no longer an idea, but a fact.

Due

Daughter/son, wrapped in your survival sac,
don't get the wrong idea. That's not the world,
though you're in striking range of it. Cramped, curled,
camped like a soldier in his bivouac,
no doubt you don't know what you're fighting for.
And powerless, your infantry can't stay
the forces that are gathering. Your choice
was made for you, but you can win this war
because you have staunch allies in the fray,
who will not rest until they hear your voice
cry its victory. If worse comes to worst,
freedom will bring pain, some shell-shock trouble.
Meanwhile, Mom's belly grows like a bubble,
where all you know of life is due to burst.

Touching Down

Described in books as stages, labor blasts off
from the pages like a rocket shuttling to outer space.
But reading didn't prepare me for the lift-off I got at your birth
when you emerged headfirst, like an astronaut
on a space walk: the new-world look of your worried face,
the rubbery cord slipping out, your breathless cough
lost in the gobbledygook of us aliens. Mom became the earth
where you landed, my hands, the gravity that caught
and carried you there. In her cosmic cap
and antiseptic garb, the midwife monitored
our flawless mission. Later, tucked in the orbit
of her arms, wrapped in a towel, you beamed from your first nap
a trace of a smile—just enough to admit
the welcome greetings we were whispering you heard.

Baby's Room

The crib's padded cell cradles its felon.
Above, the mobile fates of Mother Goose
circle to the tune of Brahms' Lullaby.
On the wall, in pastels of lime and lemon
playfully squeezed of all bestial juice,
the peaceable kingdom stretches to the sky.

The drafting table in the corner charms
disasters, for on its horizontal plane
all soiled plans are cleaned and put behind.
And raring on its rug, with open arms,
a restless rocker reaches out to rein
in doubts that rouse the wrath of infant mind.

Changed here and comforted, enticed to nurse
and sleep, Baby basks in love's universe.

October Sunflowers

The daily contemplation of the sun
swelled their heads. It was a long hot summer.
Now they dangle listlessly, every one,
bowing from that great weight, looking glummer.

Stalks arch their yellowed leaves like shoulder blades
hunched over, sort of stunted angel wings:
they've given up the ghost like many things
once lifted by light's compliment that fades.

And their golden faces, favored by the love
of fawning birds and buzzing busy bees,
are pitted now, and blankly stare profound,
as they stand stooped over the destinies
that, instead of warmly blessing from above,
with bugs and worms beseech them from the ground.

Paperweights

i.

When its world was shaken,
snow began to swirl
around the boy with his sled.
Another winter wakened

under the dome.
He was leaving home
for the woods and a distant hill
to climb.

When the storm settled,
everything stood still,
held down
by what might then
get loose or lost,
like time.

ii.

It will snow, it has snowed, it is snowing—
the child is caught in the conjugation.
Before his sled he stands, gripping its rope
like a leash. Pine trees graduate the slope.

But the sled won't track his destination
down, for the boy will never finish towing
it to the top of this childhood hill.
He will never test the sled's potential.

There's not the slightest wind nor hint of cold.
Such weather, purified in memory,
is now part of what a man has his hold

on: a stocking cap, a pair of mittens.
He shakes the ball—ceding to the flurry
his vision—and wipes his self-pity lens.

Pearly Gates

At the airport, once I'm checked in,
checked over, relieved of baggage,
padded down and deemed good to go,
I search for my gate in the terminal,
where now a wonder world beckons
with enticements of destinations
like Singapore, Tahiti, old Cuzco.

Everyone sits rapt, looking forward,
with boarding pass and passport and prayer,
to what will greet them when they arrive.
On the moving walkway, in slow motion,
I'm being passed and passing by
kingdoms of pious pilgrims when I spy
my gate number and step off. Tallyho.

Poem as Map
>	*For Connie Brown*

Some make a maze in a cornfield
that you mosey through, past dead ends
and detours, to the finish line.
Others carve a circle round an apple,
so you return where you started,
but having peeled the rich rind off.

I see it as a map you've been given—
with thematic key and compass bearings,
bold and shaded colors—arrows pointing
to a destination, with background music.
I want you to feel the topography
of my thinking, its scale and gradients.

Just follow directions and don't get lost.
I hope your questions will be answered there.

Rain Stick
For David Erickson

This piece calls for the sound of rain.
The orchestra stops and the conductor
gestures to you, and you—taking
the three-feet long, 3-inch square
rectangular cylinder of Spanish cedar,
with pins of Peruvian walnut,
throat of basswood, filled with 6.75 cups
of lentils—turn the instrument over:

a cascading swishing begins
to circulate down the spiral staircase
of little dowels, bunching in the throat,
falling with a silken pattering
of drops that freshens the air with moisture
and dissipates before they hit the floor.

Riding an E-Bike at Seventy

With pedal assist and a throttle,
I shorten and flatten the hills.
I ride farther and bolder than I ever did.
Through the workhouse of the world
I visually dance, and the air parts
as I pass, not as gauntlet but
honor guard in a Tour de France.

This is the thrill you once got
breezing downhill at nine or ten
on your coaster-geared Schwinn,
embracing a freedom that wouldn't last—
but now it does, or seems to,
as if all of life's pedaling uphill
has discharged to you. Hold fast.

Scenic Views

How many times were you tugged by a sign
to follow its lead to a scenic view
overlooking a valley, an expanse
of mountain tops, a receding shoreline?

You took your photograph and drove away,
and rarely thought of it again, unless
someone mentioned a marvelous vista,
so beautiful it stirred an urge to pray.

And then you share you had that moment too,
once or twice, when you banished the thought
that having seen one view you'd seen them all,
and followed the sign to that overlook
that answered all your doubts about the world—
how its sacred grandeur invited you.

Sea Glass

Piece of a bottle that floated in the sea,
once held by lovers making a toast,
sailing on a boat to Bliss from Glee,
on a warm summer wind, courting the coast.

Spirit of the liquid that it contained,
that once was stoppered or corked or sealed,
coursing through the veins till nothing remained
but the pleasure and joy it would yield.

Part of a promise shattered into shards,
that once was transparent and bounded,
buoyed and transported on the waves' regards,
now pearly and softened and rounded:

tumbled over and over on the wide sand bed
like a body once loved and loved and loved.

Selected Bibliography

The Wind in the Willows.
The Catcher in the Rye.
Far from the Madding Crowd.
A Moon for the Misbegotten.
The Sound and the Fury.
For Whom the Bell Tolls.

How to Win Friends and Influence People.
Doormaking: A Do-It-Yourself Guide.
The Essential Vegetable Cookbook.
The Chicago Manual of Style.
Savage Beauty, A Beautiful Mind.
The Rise and Fall of the Roman Empire.

Human Development: Means and Ends.
Hope that inspires. A good that transcends.

Situations Wanted

That need improvisation or edit-
ing. Unemployed writer, experienced
in horning the bull, cutting out the shit,
grammatical, poetically licensed,
desires novel opportunities
to punctuate night with a comma moon;
with polished pen to salvage memory's
luster from the tarnish of forgetting;
to italicize the plain truth; to spoon-
feed magic from a secret place setting.
Etcetera. Imagination free,
emotion extra. Please send self-addressed
stamped envelope with honest inquiry.
References will be furnished on request.

So Much Sadness/Sorrow Coming

The brilliant colors of the fall leaves, falling.
Migrating birds and their fading music.
The sun caving in to darkness calling.

The silent playground, the empty swing.
The valiant effort but the loss's sting.
Stamps of disapproval, rejection piles.

The no that slams the door in greeting.
The no that pricks and slowly permeates.
The no that clots the heart from beating.

Wrong turns and exit signs mis-taken.
The dog's tail-wagging in the vet's sick stall.
Footsteps fainting down the hospice hall.

Wave upon wave, sorrow's surging crest.
Swear to yourself you've done your damnedest.

Symptoms

Across the window, clouds slow-motion drift
against a backdrop beatific blue.
While the country suffers pandemic flu,
I guess I'm one of the fortunate few
who doesn't need to dream to be uplift-
ed. Each day is a new phenomenon
of weather, place, and expectations.
So far the signs seem promising but cold;
I came ready to work.
                         Listen to John,
my inoculated friends. Grow old
from immunity but embrace infections.
Show symptoms of something: make that your perk.
Life is contagious if you don't ban it.
Be thankful you were made for this planet.

Throwing Out My Mother's Slides

No one wants them.
No one owns a slide projector.
Too many foreign landscapes and street scenes.
One-by-one I hold them up to the light,
hoping to see a face I might recognize.
Covered bridges and floral fountains go,
and purchased views of ancient ruins.
Something about a village school
caught her eye and she committed it
to Ektachrome. I try to imagine her
there in the dust and heat so far from home.
I try to imagine her swaying her hips
with the belly dancers I'm looking at.
But she's always behind the lens.

To the End

It's good to get to the end of things—
the spit of land that brings
you to the shore,
the rounded cul-de-sac
that turns you back.

To close the book on the last page,
and reach that age
when everything has gone before,
when present tense accents the past.
In the days' roll call, to listen last

for your name. To have the last word.
No regrets, wondering if there's more,
when you've seen and heard
it all.

Two Photos (1951, 2010)

All of us face the firing camera
as if nothing mattered, only smiles did.
I was under two, and the three of you,
in pigtails and bangs and party dresses,
could boast of six and nine and almost twelve.
Poor baby brother, I was the spoiled kid.

To reach the other photo, each had to cross
a crevasse, a chasm, a grand canyon
of sixty years. In formal dress, we clasp
wine glasses, all link arms to celebrate,
with white hair, a beard, three colored hairstyles,
surviving divorces, children, careers—
yet mostly time, that promised nothing back when
nothing mattered. But no one knew that then.

Walking the Shelter Dogs

When I walk past the adoption cages,
each dog makes a case to be the chosen,
with a bark, a jumping up, some raucous
reason to be recognized and singled out.

When emerging on a leash, each is thrilled
beyond containing, one even straining,
as he parades past his jealous neighbors
to reach the door that magically opens.

Then there's Millie, who needs to be cajoled,
even begged, to step outside her prison,
to join me in the woods, trails beckoning,
acting as if some unspeakable crime
had been committed, and her punishment
would never be long enough to do the time.

The Weight of Love

After his breakfast, he comes back to bed
to rest on my chest, all ten pounds of him,
folding his front feet under, head forward
like the figurehead of his bread-loaf ship,
rising and falling on my calm-sea breaths,
eyes focused on his destination: me.

So it is, at different times of the day,
he'll find my lap to take a nap, anchoring
safely in my bay, all ten pounds of him.
Sails furled, meaning limbs licked clean and stowed
below in their berths, he'll plot a new course
that may take him round the household world.

Then, coming about, homeward bound again,
he'll dock his precious cargo: all ten pounds.

When I Grow Up (Since You Asked)

I want to learn how to whistle
and bring all the lost dogs home,
loping, racing, jumping with joy;

and whistle while I work, nonchalantly,
not seeming just a nerd or jerk
who's consumed with being happy;

and occasionally carry a tune
in quiet moments when I'm alone
and feeling wistful or sentimental.

To pucker my lips as if to kiss you
and exhale that musical air.
It might take me years to achieve this,
but I want to whistle without doubting
that a young boy's dreams will come, running, true.

Windrose

There were more winds in the past,
and they all had names,
like Sirocco and Levant,
Maestro and Ponente—
redolent of the airs they carried.
You navigated by a compass
of raw feelings, visceral winds.

Now we say 'it's windy out.'
'Beware of the wind chill.'
Arrows circle the weather maps
unfletched. We kite our spirits
in a nameless whirlwind,
bracing their bony shoulders,
dangling a ragtag tail.

Wishing Stone

A ring of white quartz
orbits this grainy stone
beached at my feet.
I place it in my palm,
so smooth and round,
exquisitely wrought
and well-traveled.
I squeeze till it's warm.
My wish is its mission now:
to see the world before I leave it.
I throw the stone back
to the oracle ocean
and let its worshipping waves,
as they are destined to, retrieve it.

You

The mountains haven't moved because of me.
Winds rush past as in a hit-and-run.
The rain comes down regardless what I say.

The sun acknowledges my shadow
but cleverly gets me to stomp on it.
And waves wring out my footprints in their wash.

There's little evidence that I was here
among the elements or gave them pause.
The sight of me sent wild things running.

But still I idled in the sun, and felt
refreshed by rain, and let the wind clear up
the sky so I could face the mountains.

And that was how I spent my life with you.
The years were fledgling songbirds; then they flew.

Acknowledgments

Grateful acknowledgment is due the editors of the literary magazines (print and online) that published all of the poems in this book (several in different versions):

Avatar Review: "Boy in a Boatneck Shirt and Clam Diggers", "So Much Sadness/Sorrow Coming", "You"
Calliope: "Boulder", "The Good Humor Man", "The House That Jo and Martin Built", "Laundry", "Low Tide Island", "My Turn", "October Sunflowers", "Scenic Views", "When I Grow Up (Since You Asked)"
Chiron Review: "The Domino Effect"
Colorado-North Review: "Mouse Trap"
Cook's Log: "James Cook's Window"
The Deronda Review: "Breaking Points", "Selected Bibliography"
Deep Overstock: "Cremation", "Newborn"
Grey Sparrow Journal: "Filing Order", "The Foal"
Halcyon Days: "Hush"
The Healing Muse: "Meteorologic"
Heart: "Continental Divide"
Innisfree Poetry Journal: "Two Photos (1951, 2010)"
Lights: "Wishing Stone" (and photograph)
Meow Meow Pow Pow: "The Weight of Love"
Night Picnic: "A Glass of Water", "Handwriting on the Wall", "Leafcutter Ants on Parade", "Pearly Gates"
The Ocotillo Review: "Throwing Out My Mother's Slides"
The Opiate: "The Country Club Set"
Poetry Pacific: "Downsizing", "Sea Glass", "Windrose"
Poetry Super Highway: "At the Equator", "Entering Wyoming, 1961", "Less Than 1%", "Rain Stick"
Shark Reef: "Best Laid Plans", "The Letter", "Riding an E-Bike at Seventy", "Walking the Shelter Dogs", "Farewell Tour"
Sixfold: "Let Me Tell You What I Think", "Poem as Map", "To the End"
Song: "Situations Wanted"
Songs of Eretz: "Paperweights"
Torrid Literature Journal: "Giddy Up"
The Town Square: A Literary Magazine: "Cat Philosophy"
Trolley: "Symptoms"
Visitant: "The Elephant with the Bright White Toenails"
Vox Poetica: "Ancestry.Com(mon)"
WayWords: "Kindness"

**John Delaney** retired after 35 years in the Dept. of Rare Books and Special Collections of Princeton University Library, where he was head of manuscripts processing and then, for his last 15 years, curator of historic maps. He has written a number of works on cartography, including *Strait Through: Magellan to Cook and the Pacific*; *First X, Then Y, Now Z: An Introduction to Landmark Thematic Maps*; and *Nova Caesarea: A Cartographic Record of the Garden State, 1666-1888*. These have extensive website versions.

He has written poems for most of his life, and, in the 1970s, he attended the Writing Program of Syracuse University, where his mentors were poets W. D. Snodgrass and Philip Booth. No doubt, in subtle ways, they have bookended his approach to poems. His publications include *Waypoints* (2017), a collection of place poems, *Twenty Questions* (2019), a chapbook, *Delicate Arch* (2022), poems and photographs of national parks and monuments, *Galápagos* (2023), a collaborative chapbook of his son Andrew's photographs and his poems, and *Nile* (2024), a chapbook of poems and photographs about Egypt. He lives in Port Townsend, WA.

About This Book

Though only a few of these poems are standard sonnets, I have been intrigued to experiment within their fourteen lines, sometimes with rhyme and a variety of structures, while still maintaining their strong (to me) argumentative, metaphorical nature.

www.ingramcontent.com/pod-product-compliance
Lightning Source LLC
Chambersburg PA
CBHW030058170426
43197CB00010B/1578